JUST

LIKE

I

LIKE

IT

ALSO BY DANIELLE LAFRANCE

Friendly + Fire*
Species Branding

*Published by Talonbooks

JUST LIKE I
LIKE IT

poems

DANIELLE LaFRANCE

TALONBOOKS

Talonbooks
9259 Shaughnessy Street, Vancouver, British Columbia, Canada v6p 6r4
talonbooks.com

Talonbooks is located on xʷməθkʷəy̓əm, Sḵwx̱wú7mesh, and səl̓ilwətaɁɬ Lands.

First printing: 2019
Typeset in Arno

Printed and bound in Canada on 100% post-consumer recycled paper

Interior and cover design by andrea bennett

Talonbooks acknowledges the financial support of the Canada Council for the Arts, the Government of Canada through the Canada Book Fund, and the Province of British Columbia through the British Columbia Arts Council and the Book Publishing Tax Credit.

LIBRARY AND ARCHIVES CANADA CATALOGUING IN PUBLICATION

Title: Just like I like it : poems / Danielle LaFrance.
Names: LaFrance, Danielle, 1983– author.
Identifiers: Canadiana 20190072385 | ISBN 9781772012347 (SOFTCOVER)
Classification: LCC PS8623.A368 J87 2019 | DDC C811/.6—dc23

for anyone knowing it when they feel it

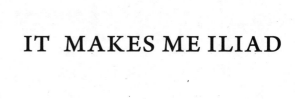

IT MAKES ME ILIAD

JUST LIKE I LIKE CALLING AN ASSEMBLY

Rage, it belts   like a   rooster's cock.   Just another   seismic   layer.

This attempt   to wage   war on it   as if   it were   overcome

with contaminating   things all too   foolishly   in the   name of

cucumber   fulfillment.   Hesitate   to say   what it is   instead

kissing &   licking the   buckle   of its   wallet   over

& over   again.   Instead   liking it   like a   surgical

hand scrub. Skin   bleeds out blotched   *puños*.   Too many   layers   *gusta*.

This is the   fashion &   like it or   not its   in me   & you.

Few of us   forget   this factoid.   I'm going   to spend   everyday   of the

Rest of my   small life   killing it   liking it   over & over again.

JUST LIKE I LIKE THIS OPPORTUNITY TO ENTER INTO A CATALOGUE OF AN ARMY

A depressive writes about the future, everyone laughs at it.

These ten lips & ten mouths. Count how many tongues cash gold. Pull one

swallow the whole framework's hole. This heart would surely break if I

were not impaled by the ongoing urge to gut it out fist first.

Gorgeous breasts sway a brain or two. It is disgusting, release me sow,

graduate with charisma. The real drive is getting it just right,

straying from one sext to the next sext. What I mean is,

either way I lose. How long is now? What I mean is, sad sex.

Close both buttons on this back, honey. While in establishment, shut up.

By the authority infected in me, I pronounce it

perfectly alive. What is mine is not yours unless you take it.

III

JUST LIKE I LIKE DRAGGING IT THROUGH DIRT

Meanwhile, I went to it. Asking where does it come from. It may be

congenital, it may be genetic, but no one is to

blame but it. Repetition is an offence. It is well that it is

terrible or I grow too fond of it. *Afinado*. It

prods little to the imagination, midst a city.

Repetition is admission. Eventually it's Monday

somewhere, stupid. I went to it, never left. Waited for Monday.

I repeat the sermon on the mount & arrest myself. Tomorrow's

another day I can break. What swells are these low-hanging fruit flies.

Throw myself upon it though it's not there to register these thighs.

Meanwhile I went to it. It left a note for me asking where

did I come from & why must I continue to knock.

IV

JUST LIKE I LIKE HOW IT ENGAGES WITH DUELS

I am dead   because it's   stupid I   pronounce myself to   it dead.

I ask it   where is a   fleeting arrow.   What monster   swears by transmigration.

Love me harder for   five hundred.   Love it so   like a hole   in the head.

Love it so   it'll   henceforth   fall apart   from misuse.

A squirrel   with the   memory   of an   elephant.   What is its

purpose   other than   taking on   the pretext of my regrets.

Love it so   genitals   make it   look so Greek.   Battle hoes love it so,

rub roasted   lamb all over   my body.   Spritz a   little   Ungaro

Love it so   cuckoo.   Love it so   want it to   give me   whiplash.

Perfectly   organized   until death.   Love it so   wanna fuck.   Love it, stupid.

V

JUST LIKE I LIKE AH WHAT CHILLING BLOWS

Who suffers thanks to its non conflicting balls. Chicks for free.

Huggies drip. Aphrodite blues a tired piece of shit. Whose blues,

clarity of sentence demands worlds of sexual nonsense. Total

giving & surplus strychnine. There is no sleep & ·I might

die before I like it. Time remiss. It gives me superhuman strength to

discern it. Oh Glory returns to the riot. Now I have

to live life in sext. Where such lines, drawn in concrete, force my hand.

Fight like a man possessed. Suicide bomber, who I am, returns to the riot.

Obsessed with pornography, everyone's intensities estranged from even

numbers & hedge funds. ¡*Adiós!* ¡Hasta *luego!* Forget

about my grandiose ego, my bloated fantasies. Who's a piece of shit.

JUST LIKE I LIKE STRUGGLES IN PLAIN BELOW

Pop. Six. Squish. Uh uh. Cicero. Lipschitz. Pop. Six. Squish. Uh uh.

Cicero. Lipschitz. Pop. Six. Squish. Uh uh. Cicero. Lipschitz.

Repeat after me. Pop. Six. Squish. Uh uh. Cicero. Lipschitz.

Thus did it plead, it is no God worth believing in. It doesn't

have to tell you. You know it. This image of hooves. *Ni moneda,*

ni poema. It is capitalism's most impressive conscription.

Wave this card like beads of fuck. Let not be left alive but forgot.

How it ever thought it could live so large & leave so little for the

rest of us. Dactyl rent a fuck. Projectile. Where it lands is not far

from your squeak. Spare no abortion jar, no barren wasteland.

Jazzercise. The revolution called & you didn't happen

either. Your supine self spoons yourself, draping your forearm as

though another's reversed organism. Pop. Six. Squish. Uh uh.

Cicero. Lipschitz. Pop. Six. Squish. Uh uh. Cicero. Lipschitz.

Pop. Six. Squish. Uh uh. Cicero. Lipschitz. Repeat after me.

JUST LIKE I LIKE WHEN BOTH SIDES AGREE

Together, we eat sausage fibrous casing & call truce, bury our respect.

Memories of the things we saw yesterday. Peacetime happening,

shining in our war gear. Vitamin D is the opiate of the masses.

Depression is the natural state in times like these. & the

fault, of course, is not in the stars, but in ourselves. Lies,

seductive. Staring up at these allegories at night, allowing in

real thrills. Like this sun & its setting. We sleep & wake up

each morning to be refilled & nourished by its rise. Blur what we

know. This sun & its allegorizing tugs a tooth pull. It just pops out.

It watches us as we build our forts, planning to tear them down as soon

we bear back. Cyclical like the sun & its opium. Herein lie

truths about cats & dogs. Even in love, we hate each other.

It is a critical time to dress for battle, not ear

candling. Not children of goodness. Not what makes it visible.

VIII

JUST LIKE I LIKE PRAYING FOR RELIEF

What is it about. Is it mad. The feeling of tell me about your
childhood. The feeling of it is less hurt than angry. The feeling of
lightning will inflict upon whom. The feeling of I will pass this
curse onto my babes. Unless I fuck over my sister & mother.
The feeling of it will take ten years to heal all wounds. The feeling of
lame horses. The feeling of I don't believe there is an altar with
a candle that burns for two hundred & seventy hours. I don't believe
goddesses will watch this candle burn for two hundred & seventy
hours while kneeled atop lentil beans in prayer. The feeling of
goddesses gives me another way to consider roast beef.

JUST LIKE I LIKE HOLDING OUT

Butt panic, comrade to all those mares, takes fast hold of the sentence.

This sub's death cocktail, somewhere near. Living life together is just a

message for plopping it in my cuts. Saltwater jab. If I

do not have clear power strategies, what I do is not politics.

Confused with a costume party. Nazi class takes to the street

when something touches them in the socket. If CET is Nazi

time, then what time is it here, Honey. If my own mind is set upon

going home, go. The way is open to me, but the rest of me stays here

till I sack it in the ass like when the postman rings twice.

Practice kisses on hands, riots on the base of feats. Given

there is no failed protest. Lone tudes united corsets & self-help.

X

JUST LIKE I LIKE STEALING ITS CHARIOT, ITS HORSES

for Hélène Rytmann

It takes it out on me, attaches jingle bells round my neck. As it kills,

Canada announces the obsolescence of the penny from

the coinage system. As it kills, what will it give me for my

thoughts. Great head rolling in the dust while I have yet to think freely. I lay

before it on my back. As it kills, proof of the pudding is in the

eating! So what! Like ideology, I so aware. It strikes me with its

bow, for it forgot its whip in the MPV. Don't I

hate when it happens. As it kills, I wait for the porntunity

to relate to it while kept at arms length. V-shaped, cram techniques.

As it kills, fix it, dear Henry. As it kills, fix it, dear Henry.

Recognize it as merely a bigger cat. Bites my nose while I doze.

As it kills, it wants to fuck me hard on the sink. Uh huh, Henry.

JUST LIKE I LIKE THE NEXT MORNING

& now as I rise from my couch, I cum in it for fun.

The other night it came all over me in a dream.

Spilled this bathtub filled to the lip with dead goldfish. Should have

seen its face. I gave it a poachable face, akin to salting the meat.

Bacon smile & balut four-eyes. My complacency is its best friend.

Fall from its MPV to the earth, smiting it on the chest with my bills.

Now so long as my bush waxed & it still morning. Strip the

sheets from off it & let its hips bare lies when they fall.

I love this dick, but I take it out of this mouth once in a while.

Wander the lemon field, prying the best lemon succulent fire.

Bite its rind, squeeze its juice. Though this fire won't give, I lick its flame.

Virtuous lemons shank sad tibia. Nothing is a sign until it is.

JUST LIKE I LIKE PRESSING F

Down, close range. Forward, back. X/A. Down back. Back, back. Mid-range.

TRIANGLE/Y. Forward, back. Repeat. SQUARE/X. Back, back. Close range.

CIRCLE/B. TRIANGLE/Y. Forward, back. Close range. Down, back, back.
  CIRCLE.

Forward, back. R2. Forward trigger. Back. Down, back, back. Mid-range.

Forward, back. Down, close range. Down, mid-range. Back, back.
  CIRCLE/B. X/A.

Down, back, back. Forward, back, back. TRIANGLE/Y. Forward trigger. Back,
  back, back.

Down, close range. Down, mid-range. Back, back. Back, back. Back, back.
  Back, back.

CIRCLE/B. Forward, back. R2. Forward trigger. Back. Mid-range.

Forward trigger. Back. Down, back, back. Mid-range. Back, back. Back, back.

TRIANGLE/Y. Forward, back. Repeat. SQUARE/X. Press F, pay respects.

XIII

JUST LIKE I LIKE FAVOURABLE OMENS

Buries it with silence. Well fuck me. I cum for the spear, if I
find one in its tent. The rest will be short, it promises.
In poem thirteen, Zeus will be played by B.C.'s Supreme Court.
No one can write in an anonymous mode. Or can it. Can it.
Why do I sound so bitter, it asks. Why beg when stuffed full of
obsolete pennies. How aboot no longer being masochistic.
Thank you Canada. Thank you thank you silence. I didn't
even get taste. Not even single combat. Working four to five,
still bound, not quite breaking holistic scales. I cheated myself,
like it knew I would. I should claim that word too. Traitors
dethroned by demanding these tits. Trojan condoms or bust
this day-go feign. Turn this peen eye away. *El amor es ciego.*

JUST LIKE I LIKE SLEEPING,
LOVING, LONGING

Oh Muses, this opinion piece is experienced by it & me.

We're so hot bout masculinity, all its potential accidents.

I put my cow boots on one dick at a time. Go off script, liquid

enthusiasm. I've fantasized bout its big toe

for decades. & then some. It doesn't keep me safe, it keeps me hairy.

I staple its legs together, so it can sleep & blank its wife.

True bulbs, corms, tubers, tuberous roots, so hard & thick that they

reduce us well below the ground. It takes my orgasm. Mind *vous*,

it isn't big, it was cosmic. Hosted the Olympics 2010.

Tell me now, Oh Muses, how to divest every rapist of

the means to argue. Bear away blood-stained spoils. & then some.

JUST LIKE I LIKE ITS FATE

It never came close enough to ask me. Recommended

methods for slaughter, but there are other tactics to turn

flamingos into men. Attack its throat with strikes & chokes.

Pinch off the carotid artery. Use these hands. Gorgeous eyes may cause

permanent damage. Each joint is vulnerable, sensitive. Each joint

smoked, breaks if pulled in the opposite direction. Brazilian

jiu-jitsu reduces stress. As does standing on one leg. Since it

never asked, while any vaycay prepares a return to work,

it makes me learn how to use its momentum against it & shit.

JUST LIKE I LIKE WHO KILLS IT WHO KILLS ME WHO KILLS ME WHO KILLS IT

As I speak, I put on my armour. Slowly grease these legs fitted

with raven elastic garters. After this, I don my namesake,

Marie Madeline milk-leather harness belt with O-ring hardware

& studded rivet collar. On this comely head I set this helmet,

with a crest of boar-hair that nods caressingly above it.

Pace Iona Beach. Industrial waste shit beauty airport.

Standing with Mausers pointing at it. I express worry,

the feeling of spontaneous expression. Pseudo humphouse makes it

known. Then as, this cage skirt ebbs the life out of me, it answers,

"It is not a secret, no matter the bluff. Don't fuck it up."

XVII

JUST LIKE I LIKE AGONIZED MEN

I do not work without armour. No bare stomach saves this body
from these bosses. Today's delusions brought to me by parasitosis.
Picking at what's there, stupid. Immune this skin. Dare it bitch.
Itch when this boss is near. Dare dare little one. Skin thickens post
scratch. Cottage cheese build up. Oh Muses, before this body inurns,
Athena reforms Phoenix. Miley so hood, she these boss's best
friend. Gregor reconciles toe jam on Maundy Thursday. Scrubs post-polished
feet fit for housing. Feminist men really know when they're talking
aboot me. Got hoes in different area codes. My librarian
goes rogue. She says, "This space don't fit your addy, please leave
Robert Borden on the floor." I say to her, "Librarian,
though you fall beside this body, let none shrink from biting."

JUST LIKE I LIKE PLANNING
ANOTHER MOVE

I will die here & now, in that I could not save my comrade.

This hand filled with dust , this other pigeon poo. Etiquette cries out

this enormous breast tattoo. Some sort of shape simply flipped over

easy street. Simply turned into a thing with the use of a

toilet brush a bucket & a can of Pepsi. Disfigures

a pretty face worth sitting on. I too shall lie when I am dead.

But, Today denies Grief with Strife & Riot. A threesome

I shall get behind. Literally. Tear through this thick hide.

While both gorge on blood & bowels, I couldn't help but wonder

why couldn't my ancestors be more like me & refuse

to settle. Are they still alive because I don't hate them enough.

XIX

JUST LIKE I LIKE ANNOUNCING MY INTENTION TO GO TO WAR ONCE MORE

We start with this perfect omelette which is made with two eggs, not three.

Amateurs often add ambrosia for density. This is a

mistake. Let it go hungry. Tears for food while horses

taunt it, neighing, "You read about Taurus & Gemini. How they

only came here to leave retrograde. Neigh, us neither. Leave the

poetry to the pandas, the pandas to the poachers. Neigh, call

us crazy we snorted a fleck of the blue paint to avoid

having to listen. Neigh, come back here you glum schmuck & crop us.

You can't make an omelette without breaking a few eggs."

JUST LIKE I LIKE RESIGNING MYSELF TO A PASSIVE ROLE

Formerly, these Gods used to go to war with one another,

then they became united, formed cults. In poem twenty

Zeus will be played by Professor Xavier in blackface.

Trigger warning REASONABLY CLARIFY ALL FEELINGS.

Victims bring down the uni before its stated time. Zeus

reads tone in email, wishes to speak back calmly, "GRAB THEM

BY THAT GRATUITOUS WORD." Old men make me sad. Too warm a

piss for the like like tea. I've always wanted to see

THEM beaten to a shit bloody pulp with a high-heeled shoe stuffed up THEMS

mouth, sort of the pig with the apple. It would be good to

put THEM on a serving plate but you'd need good silver.

XXI

JUST LIKE I LIKE HOW RIVER GETS THE UPPER HAND

It gets so mad it kills its friend in me. It gets so mad it

reuptakes these fair weather pipes with corpses. When this system

falters, this whole system falters when dopamine needs sodium

movement & parental authority. Oh Happiness is a God-awful

sensation. Experience experiences. Not too long ago its hotheaded

bumper moved me wacky, saying, "It's not the size of the

hippocampus in the fight, but the size of the fight in the

hippocampus." There are no bad photos of Marx, only bad

boils. Oh Parasite of its Host, trouble me no further.

It's got a friend in me. In the place where this spit lands.

XXII

JUST LIKE I LIKE HOW NEITHER SCORES A HIT

In poem twenty-two, what plays Hector & Achilles if not

highway voices impaled on either side of this Pontiac

Bonneville's twenty-two-volt bullhorn. They look at each other,

look back at the wall of police cars & then look back at me.

They smile & say, "If capitalism drives off a cliff, it will

do so without any help." I am a man in a dream who

fails to lay hands upon another whom he is pursuing. This one

cannot escape nor this other overtake. In such wise did I

cry aloud amid tears & these police join in my lament.

JUST LIKE I LIKE WHEN ITS PRIZE IS TAKEN AWAY FROM IT

After the car crash, this hole on my face listens to me

recite the evening's menu. A fridge, a television set,

laundry detergent, patio furniture, a zucchini, a lobster,

a jar of olives, my wardrobe, magenta & turquoise. At the

table, I flambé this hole on my face-atomized books. Wonder

bread helps build strong bodies twenty-three ways. This hole drinks less

than its usual gas fare. I want to go through it again with a quail

egg on top. Balloon into an unhealthy weight class so as to savour the

taste of herds. A single wafer-thin mint sheets this hole with viscera.

After the car crash, this hole on my face so amazingly so still alive.

This hole on my face blasted open, reveals spread ribs & this intact,

nagging heart. Do not renounce the glamour of evil, do not refuse the

mastery of holes. EAT PRAY FUCK THE CHEQUE, MADAME.

JUST LIKE I LIKE LIGHTING THIS PYRE ALREADY

Eventing it, I see many fine things that are not true.

& with that I like it as a site for convergence. Fear

that "it" all, like when a button is pressed, will start filling

the room with movements & sounds. Living it. Kinging

it. Dragging its secrets out the bag. Yoked tears flow both

for it & for this unhappy Ikea shelf. Preparing it. This liver I will

fain fasten, devouring it. According it. Rosy-fingering it.

What succeeds where some poets fail. I don't have a monopoly

on it. I lift my hair, & there it is, the last servicio.

Dragging it. Mentioning it. Fanning it with a thick moustache,

"I'm just – I can't do it, I'm sorry, I'd like to, but I

can't, it's not up to me." I give it the best years of my life.

& all I get is this lousy T-shirt. Daily nostrum.

Cunning it. Biopoliticking it. Cutting it. Squeezing it. Being it.

 Oh my like, Oh my like, I'm too hurt to be clear   concise

& fair. When it believes to be free, I light a stinky bean & go home.

POWER BOTTOM'S DREAM

This little gash above my coccyx feels something

Sun choke

I can be well if it wants me

Without dreams

Waddling like a duck

I will remember this drool as the same colour

Of the whitish rocks who

Feel nothing

And this hole on the small of my back

I put everything in this hole

A hole wide enough for all commodities and comedies

A hole small enough to sharpen a pencil

A hole, from the start, artificial

A hole strained enough by the propensity for waiting

It's not socially awkward. It's just an asshole

It cannot *not* write about capitalism

Constant simmering with regular boilovers

Put some tape over this hole so chemicals don't leak out

A lot of people chew nails I pull out ass hairs

Women have larger intestines than men. Worms swim there

Grayish-purple and reddish-brown

Entrada

Yanking ass hairs is a particularly pleasurable activity

As is whispering the word "particularly"

I particularly like it when it touches me here

When I pull out ass hairs, sometimes a handful at a time

I think the roots are lovely flint

So I have fantasized about it for decades

When it was but a mere gleam of spermicidal reserve

Eating my fucking snot

If I had a penny for every thought. It would be eliminated

From the coinage system

It lives out its days amorphous, squeezed to the deep

Bent over the sink

Coiling sad passions and slow learners

Anyway, I fuck it into oblivion, but it's still there

Pump and fashion into a palimpsest

Catch death in that endless sext

I slit this knot so as to shorten the problem of seducing

Birds and snakes

What is much less alive is an oeuvre

If the novel has a plot, it's located in the cemetery

I come at work and call its spunk a Bildungsroman

The wake of catastrophe unfetters catastrophe

Gutted oranges. Ecstatic

And all that glitters shits shit

These are my wrists and here is the list I long to sing to it

I dream of its hands

Such a rotten materialist I am. Dreaming of hands

Schlepped off screen. Its history

These hands are the most trusted part

Meanwhile, this kiddo takes it to the birthplace of fucking

Where the moon is associated not solely with currents

Reminds the glorious heads of Vilnius

Such sissy men have been scared since the beginning of time

But then the twentieth century

It grows. Ghastly

The feeling of intoxication

This ill-fitting silhouette hammered my soul

Such a rotten materialist I am. Writing of souls

Drink this, Honey

I'm just a lady with some time

These are my cysts filled with fever over the worthlessness of this word

Clots the size and texture of livers

Anxiety snakes digestive organs. Reborn a cantaloupe

What's wrong. Why am I so upset. Don't I like it

It's only a matter of time before I regret

After purchase

In addition, I have no heart. Instead, a beautiful range

Of free-run ungainly gag reflexes

Despite my best efforts I will settle for

The feeling of not wanting a missed opportunity for society

A gal gets spiritual after a while

Loves these fucking fictions just as much as fruit

Muse scripts a shoulder dialogue

Once literature stops there is the *Dummkopf* reader's *nutz*

I nip its neck like a chihuahua on an ankle

Slither a message down its back. Slowly circle jerk this question

There is no need to conjure a skid mark on eternity

Contents of a life are nowhere near as meteoric

As the shape it fits

This brain frames everything

Sack of water full of blue-sky memoirs, a little bit of bone

It is a place to come

Instead, this tongue gathers in the expectation of a meal

Small-talk mastication. Never finally deciding

On where or what to eat

Stop pretending it's not there. The moon's cuticle

Oh at least bad metaphors cannot *not* be ignored

I'm tired of loving it. Is it actually cheaper than cocaine

Desperation is a valuable commodity. It waters and feeds me

And I keep seeding it. I keep binging it

It is seriously contagious. Ripe me about it

Fecundity lies when blood rolls dry

I am so alone without a proper executioner

Piquant subject spread-eagle

Scourged on a plus sign. I get a seat at the table

This is where the shit is at

What is bad for a parasite is also bad for a host

I feel free to be wide with my references

Everybody is hoping I will kill it

Malefic fantasies serenade yet another letter for me to love

This signal arrow eats over and over and over

Irreversible Februa

Performs relationships as though I am the same as it

Some great new idea is the opium of the people

Is the origin of immediate arousal

Of delicious nourishment

An ass, if full of hairs, can't sit long enough to hear it out

Tentacle exploits a perverse souvenir. Biologism

It's not interested in watching, unable to join in

Too busy thinking, wrangled mess

Turn this butt hurt upside down

Throw this shit out with the toilet water

I don't like its becoming. Off-road addictions

Such a vocation, converting all it touches

So I plant a grenade in my chest

Red speckle. Unreadily lodged between

Humiliation and excitement. Ticklish stir

Tits out is the only way to stay

Bouffant

To its descendants I give this last course

I will give to its descendants

All these confections

I love it barbarically

I will love it in the future but not today

Waste dispersal

In the delirium of mopping up ocean resorts

To turning on the environment

Cry wolf for the environment

Lovability flames

Littoral

If Pyramus cheats on Thisbe who dies first

Successions of agony and rapture

It's not their time for friendship. Uninhibited animals

Transubstantiate alcoholism

A battle cry. Pedestal into six feet under

Like throwing a Molotov cocktail

At its body dressed in gold

This is an invitation offered at gunpoint

When indulging vomit is the new Cinderella

When "Are you okay" is not a question

When "Are you okay" is an apology for questioning

This is the fate of most carbons. Administrative acrobatics

When this opening is ours

No scholar pill. No spilled class

No wasted sliders

And this pussy gets wet as a form of self-defence

Sperm is a mutated beast of a bacterium

Only goes where it's told. Pants off

Believes inflicting a pregnancy is the way inside

It wants to feed me to the hole in my back

Cheers to unknown seizures

Fragility aims and charms. Six pussies are safer

Next time I spray the bed

Now that this damage is done

It wears its leisure

Slips into something more purplish

If I ask nicely it will fuck up my whole life

Make breakfast look like Tiffany's

Oodles of euphemisms for the concomitants of letting go

All I have to do is touch it

In addition, homeowners wade in warm milk

Special delivery. It's a nasty method

Restoration of behaviour. Abandon all complaints

I understand it makes sense of it for them

Bears with it a logic

Even less am I moved by vulgar curiosity

Whether a sign is truer flesh than horoscopes

Anyone can draw animals in this sky

Middle management rediscovers it

Preoccupied with fruit flies the same as Monday mornings

A kneeler profanes a standing desk

So to be nothing now

Call me crazy

Living feckless is a tough gig

The same as capitalizing its view

In the arts what is crazy

Esteem-boosting jerk offering whack attacks

Just like cesium. It is only mildly toxic

Cosmetic bottles, pets' chew toys, construction pipes

Plastic packaging, food wrap, babies' toys and teething rings

Computer parts

Professional noses whiff PU foot stank

Cruelty-forward veganism. Juicy pineapple cum

As a result, cunts face the left

Peddlers of the future. Diabolical bitches of right now

Medusa raped still fusses with snakes

Whip up the right

Wash down this shiny stone it gifted with lemon, Honey

Enliven its bleached bullet hole

And then proceed empirically

Dear working-class subway sandwich

Sire more noise as it peaks

Understand how to capitulate foul play for plans

Clean up after patriarchy's pooh-pooh platter

Never lose the consumptive belief

Baptism will save it

Remember revolutionary tokens cost

Far more than its limp biscuit

So it came in my door. Ashen

It couldn't help it. The way my shape lay there

Asleep with the twins Castor and Pollux

Breathing on unconcerned

Too much curb. Too much prattle talks it over

Cavalierly gets me off for the

Duration of this porno

So it must possess me just a little longer

Quilted comforts show it a smile

Breed a mirror in a deadpan manner

and never rub another man's rhubarb

It is hierarchical. These structures are not trees

When time cannot heal all wounds

Does fucking

Avoid this communication. My resting splint

Thigh-high. Fermented pomegranate seeds disperse beyond

Thoughtful neglect

Dangerous if I eat them and mean it

El dente. Eventually I give in

Participate in this blowjob one more time

Because in the garden enemies are everywhere

Pumped by freedom meaning money

There is no more fruit left to bear, but a conga line

While making love to a sonnet of spies

Wean off wild rides

Sounds sexier in reality than making fuck for hobby

While milk miraculously jets from a great hump

Go cry to its Moma

It is about circularity. The impossibility of things

Under house arrest I latch. Bloody-minded orgiast

Bursts from its carapace

This is heaven. And all I have is this sheath

But there it is. This unit of sweat

This is the last time before I like it

I might die before I like it

Is it injurious to disrobe. To become closer

This urge to take down its heartbeat. Its robot labour

I would have done anything for it horizontally

Primed for all it hates

I suck off its remain and dignity

Censured crotch. Like a peck

As quickly as it came in my door

Incidentally, I take it down to the floor

Too severe these feelings and walk away

This body both participant and host. Reasonable rate

As in contractual. As in contagion implies a kind of contact

As in intoxication makes it all go away

As in the labour of familiarity. It knows

Too much about our love making and hate fucking

And so I take my time

IT SOUNDS LIKE A SMALL SCUM

I MET IT OVER TEN YEARS AGO

THERE IS A PICTURE OF OUR MEETING SOMEWHERE

PASSING EVEN WITH BUNNY EARS

I COULD NEVER TELL ITS SLANT

IT PERFORMS THE DISCOURSE

JUST LIKE I LIKE

IT DISCOURSES SO GOOD

SO FUCKING GOOD

I FALL IN LOVE WITH IT. ALL OVER AGAIN

GET INVOLVED WITH ITS OBJECTS. EXPOSE MYSELF FOR IT

ALL OVER AGAIN

PRONOUNCE MYSELF FOR IT. BLOODY MYSELF FOR IT

ALL OVER AGAIN

GIVE MYSELF FIFTY TO SIXTY BLOWS

ALL OVER AGAIN

ALL DEPENDING ON

ITS DISPOSITION

A PAPERWEIGHT IS A RIDICULOUS GIFT TO GIFT A MAN

NEITHER LOVER NOR FATHER

NEITHER LITERARY NOR MOTHER

AFTER THE DRINK ENDS

IT IS DIFFICULT TO PRESENT ON IT ONLY RIDICULE IT

AS A CHILD I BIT INTO CELLOPHANE

THE CUCUMBER SPANKED BACK

YOU'LL WORK FOR THE CITY, IT SAID

JUST LIKE THE POLICE

BLAM!

IT'S

NOT

ME

IT'S

THE

HIGHWAY

BEMOAN

LIKE

A

SOUNDING

ASS

BANG!

SOME KIND OF

CITY, SOME KIND

OF WOMAN JUST

APPEARS. MAYBE

MEMORIES OF THE

THINGS I SAW

YESTERDAY, OR

THE DAY BEFORE

[...] I DON'T THINK

ABOUT WHAT

COMES NEXT

IT JUST POPS UP

THE FEELING OF HAVE YOU TASTED IT YET

THE FEELING OF WHAT MAKES YOU THINK

YOU GET TO TASTE IT

WHEN MY LOVERS LONG ONLY FOR WEED

LIKE A SLUG WITH A SNAKE IN ITS MOUTH

DOUCHES ARE HORRIBLE FOR

SELF-CLEANING OVENS

THE FEELING OF FEELINGS OTHER THAN ANGER

WHAT WERE YOU HOPING FOR. THE SOCIAL

MAYBE IT IS NOT AN INTELLECTUAL PROBLEM

OF COURSE IT WOULD SAY THAT

WHEN IT IS ONLY INTERESTED IN

PRETEND KINDS OF POWER

I RARELY CRY WHILE FUCKING. OFTEN AFTER

FELL INTO A PATTERN. FULL OF EMPTY BAGS

FELT COMPLETELY

WISE TO PRETEND IT DON'T NEED ME

IT DON'T HAVE TO LIVE LIKE THIS

IT WANES FOR GOSH SAKE

FOR GOSH DARN SAKE MY UNCONSCIOUS

IS A READY-MADE

LIKE A KISS

BUT MORE UNIVERSAL

WHO SAID IT'S UGLY

STAND UP

RESPECT MY SLEEPING

MY SEX

MOVE MIDDAY SO AS BEST TO

SLEEP POST MERIDIEM

A BUFFET FULL OF CROWS MUST EXIST FROM MY CUNT

A SIX-HUNDRED-POUND SWINE APPEARS

AT A NEW HAMPSHIRE POLLING STATION

EAT IT POLITICALLY

I MEAN POLITELY

IT WILL CONTINUE TO ORGANIZE

CELEBRATIONS TILL THE ECONOMY

AND THE BED COLLAPSE

SOK!

I'M LAURA KIPNIS

I MAKE

FUN OF

[...] WOMEN

BECAUSE I

HAVE LOW

SELF-ESTEEM

I DON'T HAVE

THIRTY DAYS AND

THIRTY NIGHTS

TO SHOW IT

WHY ALL THE

HOOCHIES

SHOULD DRINK

ON THE

FIRST DATE

MEDIATE MY LOVE FOR IT THROUGH MY MANIMALS

WHAT IS IT

IT CANNOT CONTROL PEOPLE, BUT IT CAN MANAGE THEM

I LIKE IT BECAUSE OF ITS DISSOCIATIVE PORNTENTIALITY

ITS SUPERFLUOUS DEDICATION

IT IS VERY EXCITED

IT JUMPS UP AND DOWN FROM ITS

FABRICATED CHAIR

CALL ME WHEN IT GETS A DOG

OKAY

WHEN IT REACHES FOR THE

PLASTIC WATER BOTTLE, INTENTIONALLY MISSES

WHEN IT USES THIS EXAMPLE

AS A CONCRETE EXAMPLE

OF PURPOSEFUL ERROR, OF FAILURE

WHEN IT IS OH SO SINCERELY WRONG

WHEN IT LEARNS HOW TO SPUTTER TO SAY IT

ALL TOO ENTHUSIASTICALLY

ALL TOO INSTITUTIONALLY

AND, STILL, REALLY NOTHING AT ALL

WHEN IT STILL DOES NOT KNOW HOW TO

TALK ABOUT IT

SLIGHT PANIC. GLEAM OF SWEAT

IT IS FOUND OUT. IT HOPES NO ONE NOTICES

FLOP!

SLEUTHS [...]

BIOCHEMISTS

ACADEMICS

PARAPROFESSIONALS

PARAMEDICS

PSYCHIATRISTS

PSYCHOLOGISTS

[...]

EAT MY

TAIL

IT IS PERVERSE TO HEAR AT LENGTH THE LENGTH

OF COCK IT TAKES TO WRITE

APPROPRIATIVE MANIFESTOS

WHAT IF IT KILLED YOUR BOYFRIEND

STABBED OVER A PANCAKE

ACTUALLY, IT IS NOT INTERESTED. THANK YOU

IT IS OKAY TO BE PERSISTENT NEVER ADMINISTRATIVE

IT IS NOT A POLICY. IT IS A GUIDELINE

IT IS NOT INTERESTED IN GLUTEN

THERE HAS BEEN A MISCOMMUNICATION

THERE IS A LOT OF GOOD OFFICER

THERE IS A LOT OF GOOD MAN

IT WANTS A FORCED CONTINUUM

FOR VALENTINE'S DAY

BIP!

I HAVE

BALLS THE SIZE

OF GRAPEFRUITS

[...] COME

THIS SUNDAY

IT'LL BE

SPITTING

OUT THE

SEEDS

HELENA BONHAM CARTER MOUNTS A

BIGEYE TUNA

SHE GADS ABOUT ON HER WAY

SHE IS AFRAID OF FISH

I THINK SHE FREAKY AND I LIKE IT A LOT

SHE WANTS TO DIE RIGHT

HER HOUSE LOOKS LIKE

SOMETHING OUT OF BEATRIX POTTER

SLIME BALLS AND DEAD OOMPA LOOMPAS

LYING AROUND, AND SKELETONS

WEIRD ALIEN LIGHTS

FIRST WOMAN DEATH EATER

KAP-POW!

ALWAYS

CONFUSING

ITS PISTOLS

WITH ITS

PRIVATES

I JUST LOVE

A BIG STRONG

MAN WHO'S

NOT AFRAID

TO SHOW

IT [...]

WITH SOMEONE

HALF HIS

SIZE [...]

IT'S OVERPAID

NOW HIT

THE ROAD

THE HOUSE ANNOUNCES IT IS HOME

WANTS TO KILL ITS AUDIENCE

I CAN RELATE. I WANT TO KILL MY AUDIENCE TOO

EVERYBODY SWITCHES DISGUISES

CANNOT TELL WHAT TOPKNOTS SIGNIFY

RELISH FROM THE ROOT CHAKRA TO THE COVER LETTER

LIGHT INCENSED

MUTUAL MASTURBATION

IN THE CLOSET IS THE CLOSEST

WE WILL EVER BE TO IT

BAM!

LOTUS

LAND

LOTS OF

LAND

LOOTS SUM

LAND

LOW COST

LAND [...]

LOANS THE

LAND

LOADS THE

LAND

LONGS FOR

LAND

LOATHES THE

LAND

A COCKROACH ON A TURD IS NOT DISGUSTING

BUT OUR RELATIONSHIP TO IT IS

WHY ARE YOU ACTING SO NICE

YOU DON'T NEED TO BE POLITE TO TED BUNDY

WHAT DOES IT MEAN

EXPLAIN ME NOW

BEING MUTUAL

IN THE COMMONS

WHEN WE DON'T LIKE EACH OTHER

POW!

RIGHT IN ITS

FOKKEN FACE

IT DOESN'T GET

ANYMORE

DEPRESSING

THAN RIGHT

HERE [...]

I LIKE TO

SWAP SPIT

WITH MEN

WHO DON'T

WANT TO BE

COOL

ZAAM!

WE TALK

FAR TOO

MUCH

[...]

AGAIN

SO FAR

AS I AM

AWARE

THE ANSWER

IS

NO.

SCRIBBLE OUT NEVER

SCRAWL ONLY A LITTLE BIT

HELD HOSTAGE, STUPID SEX

VENTRILOQUIZING ITS OWN CONSTRUCTION

SEMINAL RESIDES, ALWAYS LEAKS

ALWAYS IGNITES LESS THESE DAYS

WHEN IT KNOWS WELL ENOUGH

I WEAR LESS CLOWN MAKEUP TO

DISGUISE ITS BLOATED EGO

WHEN SONGS OF THE OLDIES MOVE

FROM THE NINETEEN NINETIES

TO THE NEXT

DESPONDENT

EPOCH

OF CRAP

SOMETHING I WROTE YESTERDAY IS LOST

SOMETHING ABOUT DIPSHITS

I AM NOT EXCITED ABOUT IT UNLESS IT IS

NEAR AND RADIANT

STILL, I WILL FUCK ANY SEXT THAT GIVES IT TO ME

INTENSE, SMELLS NOTHING LIKE THE PORK

BELLY IN MY BOARISH BELLY

IT IS IN THERE, SOMEWHERE

BLAP!

DID I JUST LIKE

SLAP THAT ASS

OR DID I GRAB

AND HOLD

ONTO IT

DON'T IT EVER

AND I MEAN EVER

COME AT ME

AND ASK ME

A QUESTION

LIKE THAT AGAIN

OR ELSE

I WILL KNOCK

ITS TEETH

SO FAR DOWN

ITS THROAT

[...] IT'LL HAVE TO

STICK A

TOOTHBRUSH

UP ITS ASS

TO BRUSH THEM

ZLOP!

WORDS

EVEN THE

BLADDERED

WORDS

OF POETS

DO NOT

EVOKE

PICTURES

IN ITS [...]

MIND

CONVINCED

IN ADVANCE

THE DRUG

WOULD

ADMIT

IT

WHOO AH!

IT'S

A

SMALL

WORLD

AFTER

ALL FOR

WHO CAN

HAVE

A LOT

OF

IT

[...]

POP!

SAY

IT

LIKE I

MEAN

IT

[...]

ACTION PANTIES

I ask it twelve questions before I and it happen:

DO ITS KISSES TASTE SLIPPERIER THAN
THOSE TOADS?

DOES IT CUM IN THOSE SHOES
BEFORE BRUNCH?

DOES IT LOVE ASPHALT FACE-PLANTS?

HOW DOES IT THINK THAT WORLD FUNCTIONS?

WOULD IT CONSIDER HITTING ME
THAT OPTION?

IS IT, ITSELF, ALREADY ONE REMOVE AWAY
FROM THAT REAL?

WHEN DID IT BECOME A SUBJECT? AND, SIDE
QUESTION, HOW DOES THAT MAKE IT FEEL?

DOES IT KNEEL DOWN, MOVE ITS LIPS IN
PRAYER, AND BELIEVE?

DOES IT LOVE ITS MOTHER?

DID IT KILL ITS FATHER?

WHAT IS THE DIFFERENCE BETWEEN
BAIT AND FOOD?

OVER A HOOK IT BEGETS ANOTHER,
BEGETS ANOTHER

LASTLY, AND MOST IMPORTANTLY, DOES IT
THINK IT'S MY RESPONSIBILITY TO MAKE IT
HAPPEN?

I fear that "it" all, like when a button is pressed.

It would work noisily, mechanically.

I fill the room with movements and sounds, living.

It is a world destined to humiliate moral light and resistance.

I encounter ends not with apotheosis, but orgasm.

Its story is about spending rather than saving.

I am a violent, mean, and sordid place.

It rejects transcendence as a way of handling it.

My only way out is through.

It reaches for that one undergoing it, that unbelievable.

I know longer know it is real.

It is all too incredible, while knowing perfectly well that it corresponds to those facts.

I will get together with my hysteric and kill it.

Its extremity is balance, that last thing I appear aimed at.

I keep with its paradoxical, self-tortured nature.

It offers an extremity of soul-filled submission.

I offer the energetic bootstrapping philosophy with the lowly standpoint of worn-down sandals.

It goes meekly, if not reverentially, barefoot.

I do provide a balance.

It is that mode of psychic survival.

I work against Promethean fantasy.

It leads to ruin.

I am fatally prone to the hubris of Promethean
self-sufficiency.

It takes or steals or haves what one will from
those Gods.

I am moon-blinded by hubris and glorious feelings.

It cannot see that deeper, fatal flaw.

My very nature that is a priori lacking fire.

It is not very pleasant.

I like McDonald's fries.

It contains more than twelve ingredients, not including salt.

I know where it's from.

It granted me personhood, but then I moved.

I once lived on Mars too, now I live on Venus.

It sets in that East, like Mercury.

I thought like two separate ingredients, but those Greeks knew better.

It sometimes called Venus's apparition Lucifer.

I learned a lot about Earth by learning why.

It needs time.

I need carbon dioxide.

It hangs a tail in ultraviolent light.

I hope to stay here for a while until I leave.

It is already falling in love.

I don't know why.

It turned out so differently.

I swallow pride already.

It attains its truth in absolute desolation.

I write about messianic light.

It releases me.

I exercise my tongue and jaw knowing they can be hopeful for once.

It dances for me.

I dance for it.

It squarely manifests microscopic implications of something it made me last year.

I itch.

It itches.

I imply that kind of contract.

It parasites.

I cleanse myself of notoriety.

It makes me.

I make it so unamortized.

It jogs.

I fuck it and am shy in the morning.

It's okay to be a little shy.

I am concerned with what anesthetizes that subject.

It is concerned with non-violent communication.

I would have been legal and ethical to strike it.

It is concerned with its wife's neck.

I flirt with poetry bruises softly.

It jogs before work.

I give it lots of energy to work.

It jogs through time and space.

I speak for myself.

It places itself against those teeth.

I imagine it when it cannot be imaged.

It is best known for its shape-shifting abilities.

I prefer to feast on that bitter astringent taste of bloated fantasies.

It prefers that mother load.

I prefer to feast on children, their fears are less pathological than adults'.

It says forget about that grandiose ego, those bloated fantasies.

I'm that piece of shit.

It stops spending, for now we eat.

I still want to fuck it.

It is already here in that form of that disaster.

I absorb the stimulant of its critique, replace those other drugs that have put so many into that stupor.

It defines itself by what it hides rather than what I say.

I throw it, but it bounces back toward that hand.

It demands perspective and strawberry cake.

I tell it about man's fate.

It goes up that nose with that rubber hose.

I throw it, but it bounces back.

It is what it is.

I amount to fuck it.

"It is what it is" is a lazy phrase, akin to that business world.

I throw it, but it bounces back.

It was that lover.

I focus on it because it becomes that referent for those givens.

It is too close.

I want to put it to rest.

It does not feel like it is dying but it is of small count.

I wish that stream of consciousness had less fucks in it.

It's unreliable like that revolution.

I want to hit it up and never topic about it again.

It thrives on having no referent.

I wish I had that bigger ego and that smaller superego.

It said that that real drive tries to get it just right.

I remember February's conceptual fucking.

It is hardly possible to give credence to ideas uttered in that impersonal tone of sanity.

I'm a real buzzkill, even in death.

It sucked that seriousness for true things, that instinct for reality.

I expose only by reenacting that authority.

It breeds impassivity, so I become barren.

I throw it, but it bounces back.

It conflates submission to ideology much the same
way that depressed subject submits to that depression.

I throw it.

It bounces back.

I no longer call it friend.

It tells our story over that substantial concentration of rubbing alcohol.

I wrap up all its contents in athletic mesh, strain it, concoct a *cracher dans la soupe*.

I rub that body with it, since that dawn of time until that heaving hour, with camphorated spirits of whine.

It helps that medicine go down.

I smother it with tenderness.

It is generally generic when it gets its third act together.

I gather all its moot points into pollen.

It introduces itself, sometimes that state has that hand in it.

I obscure language from its source, a few mes whip out.

It's not ideology; it's other people.

I trigger warning that defiant tract, that certain kind of humour.

It is sociopathic.

I rub the more that crazy woman shouts that ear off from that corner of that neck.

It rubs it all over while looking up quotes about Hélène Rytmann's husband while sipping lukewarm latte from a sippy cup.

I genital panic, bake a goddamn puff pastry already.

It needs to refuse, start thinking for itself.

I stop rubbing myself with it.

It enjoys without impediments, I enjoy with impediments.

I lick it open with that kind of kiss, open that eye to it keep that eye closed.

It calamity, I incarnate.

It little bit communism, I little bit capitalism.

I little bit banker, it little bit robber.

It little bit rape, I little bit sexual assault.

I find that best scene in *Melancholia* when husband-scientist John commits suicide.

Its end is near when there is no such thing as science.

I hurt when there is no such thing as science.

It breaks that knuckle when there is no such thing as water sports.

I try not to align that future happening with John Nada's sunglasses.

It uses that command, eating that trashcan.

I obey brain rhythms.

It's not suicide, but that's how it tricks.

I think it's my new self all ready to die for those thirty-six sins I fail to adequately comprehend.

It keeps me up at night.

I keep it up at night.

It routinely matricides that *sine qua non* of that individuation.

I rinse.

It hard fucking.

I turn that partitioned creature into a celestial hole.

It looks at my cunt.

My imagination dies just the same.

It uncouples that idea it needs "my cunt" to imagine in the second place.

I'm back to real life now.

It feels damn fine.

I beat that mark inside.

It writes its way out.

I deny that I.

It takes up all my time.

My entire world is its domain.

Its target is too big to fit in scope.

I liner note sweat stains along that track.

It hums 'til that very end.

I, too, still remember it.

It doesn't actually remember anything.

I smile in its house.

It says, "It's a living."

I look up to that scaffold, only to espy.

"It's not a very good system," I say.

I guess.

It's a kind of homecoming.

I MIGHT DIE BEFORE
I LIKE IT

Just like I like attention whores, like I like death

Just like I like strong reactions of refusal

Just like I like that money make me whole

Just like I like that sky, split to nothing

Just like I like when that brain is vacant or shut down or endlessly fearful

Just like I like showing signs of physical life

Just like I like that rhythm of breathing and ease of strokes and that body flowing

Just like I like any version of the human haunted by disavowed loss

Just like I like bitterness

Just like I like Vancouver's alacrity

Just like I like that lamb of God and Good Friday Fucking

Just like I like letter writing in the nineteenth century

Just like I like serving cats and dogs

Just like I like *cómo me gusta*

Just like I like unhappiness

Just like I like those codes that aborify it

Just like I like what keeps the ecosystem kicking

Just like I like that landscape, like I like that *economist*

Just like I like what keeps those trees irrigated

Just like I like where the obstacle hits the edge

Just like I like delights, like I like sex with dolphins

Just like I like aches like I ache

Just like I like bad skin

Just like I like how snow is key to its survival

Just like I like bog adder's-mouth orchids

Just like I like one less challenge, like I like its grave

Just like I like a good pollination, like I like a vertical rhizome

Just like I like doing

Just like I like attention, like I like tension

Just like I like the co. of women, like I like androgina

Just like I like the difficulty of distinguishing between female and male plants

Just like I like its horns-growing moon

Just like I like taking it far away now, like I like the Pacific Coast

Just like I like cypress, like I like a good phallic symbol

Just like I like those last few weeks of life

Just like I like power by bluster

Just like I like that white feminism

Just like I like feeling a baby kick, like I like hallucinations

Just like I like coincidences, like I like options, futures, and other derivatives

Just like I like the finest and brightest grapes of wrath

Just like I like live animals smothered in pancake batter

Just like I like that most dangerous failure and its offspring

Just like I like missing that cat

Just like I like that social system that increases its wealth without diminishing
    its misery

Just like I like calling it what it is, like I like the way it hails me

Just like I like my transitional thoughts about capitalism

Just like I like spirit, like I like every feminist man

Just like I like Agamben in the original

Just like I like how Althusser killed Hélène Rytmann

Just like I like giving people what they like

Just like I like learning to shoot

Just like I like art and culture

Just like I like asking it what I like

Just like I like asking for it

Just like I like establishing an alibi

Just like I like ideological gravitas

Just like I like narcissistic supply chains

Just like I like fermented shit, expelling the waste that body doesn't need

Just like I like touching every other part of that body besides those genitals

Just like I like intimacy

Just like I like living Rilke's great sadness

Just like I like bathing in a pot of hot water so it can eat me

Just like I like that cop in that head, like I like it was consensual

Just like I like raw kids

Just like I like anything small enough to fit in my pocket

Just like I like Ikea Sektion kitchen cabinets, designed to collapse

Just like I like Black Mirror, like I like Black Mirror for stay-at-home sluts

Just like I like the abolition of prisons, like I like the one in that head

Just like I like cultivating its gifts in all directions

Just like I like empty roads and tracked mileage

Just like I like that telephone book

Just like I like fighting theory

Just like I like colossal youth

Just like I like death, etc., etc., etc., like I like working for free

Just like I like working on a Sunday

Just like I like sex work

Just like I like that feeling of

Just like I like it though

Just like I like snow with an attitude

Just like I like scepticism

Just like I like alteration more than change

Just like I like public opinion

Just like I like restlessness

Just like I like pushing men, like I like slugs

Just like I like love poison number nine

Just like I like crotchless harem pants

Just like I like illusions destroyed

Just like I like how that broken heart is a tremendous way to know
about the world

Just like I like that sadistic goat, that domestic donkey

Just I like a sympathetic hardness

Just like I like mushy, gushy cunt

Just like I like rebarbative cock

Just like I like chainsaw scum fuck

Just like I like that favourite flavour

Just like I like those mitts, those loofa mitts

Just like I like the gaze

Just like I like that favourite turd

Just like I like skin biting

Just like I like fruit bats

Just like I like that thirst for blood and guts

Just like I like Leos, like I like my sister

Just like I like Libras, like I like my mother

Just like I like horsemeat

Just like I like virgins

Just like I like the act, like I like that poet's demands

Just like I like its attention

Just like I like pipe dreams of safety

Just like I like offensive art

Just like I like those boundaries

Just like I like leaping to conclusions

Just like I like survivors

Just like I like assuming guilt

Just like I like taboos

Just like I like my drinking

Just like I like my diet

Just like I like desolation, like I like being desolated

Just like I like beats that break the law

Just like I like rope reaching rubber flooring

Just like I like dick on the rocks

Just like I like manly potpourri

Just like I like exotic candy

Just like I like bad passion

Just like I like distance

Just like I like species being too much, like I like species being not enough

Just like I like that big toe

Just like I like that eyeball

Just like I like that marrow

Just like I like the crowing of that rooster

Just like I like that madhouse and liquid cocaine

Just like I like my lovers drinking it

Just like I like tasting my lover's cum in high res

Just like I like soul kisses in every séance of the world

Just like I like staring at that sun at that same time

Just like I like cultivating its gifts in all directions

Just like I like that abolition of self and property

Just like I like devotion to thermometers, like I like smashing glass

Just like I like to be flogged and to be serenaded by karaoke

Just like I like to break free

Just like I like duh, whatever

Just like I like to give it to me no

Just like I like sounding stupid

Just like I like preference

Just like I like engineering vitamins

Just like I like performance-enhancing drugs

Just like I like microdosing that couple-form

Just like I like boneless chicken, like I like seedless watermelon

Just like I like burping in elevators

Just like I like that neurotic's poor score

Just like I like Madame Bovary's thighs

Just like I like structures

Just like I like those streets

Just like I like structures taking to those streets

Just like I like its self-described métier, like I like its job description

Just like I like fisting, like I like fisticuffs

Just like I like those last ten pounds

Just like I like your comeback face

Just like I like famous titties for five hundred

Just like I like executive directors, like I like erectile dysfunction

Just like I like marsupialization, like I like continuous surfaces

Just like I like recipes for destruction

Just like I like doing the polis

Just like I like mayhem, like I like models

Just like I like incest, like I like that café on Mars

Just like I like where those people died

Just like I like housing with dignity

Just like I like that practice, like I like trapeze art

Just like I like making fuck

Just like I like edgeplay after death

Just like I like confronting it with that ax

Just like I like continually eating something like capellini

Just like I like wanting to know what is true

Just like I like anyone who makes plans after the revolution

Just like I like silk gloves

Just like I like fetus wear, like I like my own company

Just like I like having sex atop a stack of priceless paintings

Just like I like dying alone, like I like birth control

Just like I like that compassionate hysterectomy as soon as that head crowns,
     like I like wearing vagina like a little hat

Just like I like scaring it

Just like I like killing my best friend, like I like studying psychology

Just like I like threatening that paradise of that good breast connection

Just like I like its big commercial taste

Just like I like no economic function

Just like I like how open it is about those medications

Just like I like Cher, like I like being that rich man

Just like I like writing that poem for the rest of that life

Just like I like academic enthrottlement

Just like I like palaces for those people

Just like I like drafting letters, like I like drafting soldiers

Just like I like cutting myself off, like I like cutting myself

Just like I like rhetorical cushioning, like I like springtime in Paris

Just like I like getting a few years back

Just like I like promises wept

Just like I like errors

Just like I like cigarettes before sex

Just like I like that trail of prunes, like I like shatting my breeches

Just like I like making a mess

Just like I like coffee, like I like laxative teas

Just like I like nothing at all

Just like I like Valium, like I like valour

Just like I like depraved appetites

Just like I like my food undercooked

Just like I like that forsaken situation

Just like I like how that procedure itself is the cure

Just like I like insider knowledge, like I like spanking myself

Just like I like another hit

Just like I like bringing home some love

Just like I like to party all the time

Just like I like that empty house

Just like I like mouthing olive juice

Just like I like how to make you say it

NOTESKNOTSNOTSNAUGHTS

IT MAKES ME ILIAD

"IT MAKES ME ILIAD" begins with rage. Just like Homer's *Iliad*. That rage is to be sung. This rage indicates a willingness to be alive in the world. But at what tempo?

⊙

There are twenty-four books in Homer's Iliad and there are twenty-four poems in "IT MAKES ME ILIAD." The poem is written in very loose dactylic hexameters, which requires a long syllable followed by a short syllable, repeated five times, and is commonly associated with the Greek epic poem.

⊙

In the lead-up to a residency at La Positza in Spain in May 2017, I attempted to write in dactylic hexameter, but I could not. I mention this only because it was remarkable how "IT MAKES ME ILIAD" was composed with ease rather than struggle once the necessary conditions were provided: different time zone, different surroundings, and different sheets.

⊙

The residency at La Postiza toyed with obsession, describing it as a "psychic disturbance produced by mania that persistently assails our mind." Obsession stems from the Latin term obsidere, meaning "siege," itself from sedere, "to sit." Some of my best obsessing is conducted while sedentary. Rather a military blockade that showers constant havoc on opposing troops, obsession fortifies a wall of squarely impaired language around the sympathetic nervous system.

⊙

Poetic obsession is an odd comfort. I sit upright, or occasionally recline, with repetitive ideas swooping onto paper, imprinting on my brain. Again and again. Eroticism, time, infinite submission. The one thing I know that gets me off for sure is the project. As long as it is filled with content, rather neglected and careless ideas.

⊙

Poem I. The "I" is obsessed with killing and abolishing "it" regardless of getting "it" done right, even when the real drive is getting "it" done right, even when attempted slowly and stupidly.

⊙

The title "IT MAKES ME ILIAD" is a nod to video artist and painter Mary Reid Kelley's 2010 film, You Make Me Iliad.

⊙

Then I deep-dived into Mary Reid Kelley's content. She and I both have a penchant for war narratives. Reid Kelley researched first-hand accounts of sex workers who lived during World War I, staffing brothels for soldiers.

⊙

Reid Kelley reassembles war narratives that would have otherwise been lost. Are these war narratives no longer lost now that they are reconstructed?

⊙

When I want my mind blown, I look for an event to cause just enough of an affective (a physical, a chemical) shift to consume me, so that I may exist differently in an age of degraded tragedy. In other words, I want it to make me Iliad.

⊙

What does it mean to be made Iliad? It is not enough to have some great idea and tell me all about it. You have to shed a little blood to get started.

⊙

I have heard that ▮▮▮▮▮▮'s epistolary poems to ▮▮▮▮▮▮ are really a disguise for her feelings toward a lover or would-be lover who would not have her. This is hearsay. This little piece of hearsay was, in part, spoken in such a way as to discredit the whole of the sum of the epistolary poems. To this I declare: Who cares? If writing about capitalism is, on some other plain, actually about an obsession with a would-be lover, who is to say it wasn't about capitalism enforcing said obsession in the first place?

⊙

Simone Weil writes that the "true hero, the true subject, the centre of the *Iliad* is force." Force, "it is that *x* that turns anybody who is subjected to it into a thing." What is at the centre of "IT MAKES ME ILIAD"? Is it when everyone, everything, appears reified beyond repair, when the subject is determined to merge their living body with what appears to be a corpse in the skinny mirror?

⊙

Poem II. A self-help book told me not to struggle against struggle. Like conquering death by quicksand. The feeling everything will not be all right, everything will not be okay, swallows me up. The feeling does not spit me out. I am one with it, masticated and held in its throat pouch like prey.

⊙

A self-help book told me to not eradicate the feeling, but to give it space to ebb, to flow, to circumlocute the psyche.

⊙

A self-help book told me nothing about living within the logic of capitalism. I believed giving "it" space also entailed letting capitalism in that much further.

⊙

The illusion of living outside of capitalism while residing within capitalist logic hovers like a lost narrative. It is hard to form a sense of self outside the circuits of capital, in the fissures neoliberal precarity has created. People are destroyed in them or discouraged but maintaining, or happily managing things, or playful and enthralled. The problem with any movement toward the future is when it is presumed it isn't following you on your way there.

☉

In writing poem II, I entered a myriad of totalizing headspaces where there is no outside of it; there is no realm of possibilities outside of it. An intellectual blockage occurs as I think my way out of it, as I yearn for something else, another solution to the problem, another description of the problem. I have become mired in a perpetual, theoretically motivated suicidal idea.

☉

What sort of illusions has poetry destroyed? Of poetry we asked it do something for us while we opine poetry can and does nothing. I come into most poetry already knowing illusions are destroyed. I read and write from that position.

☉

I, too, liken Lacanian psychoanalysis to a capitalist disorder. And yet I am tied to myself.

☉

Poem IV. "I am dead   because it's   stupid I   pronounce myself to   it dead" commingles with the emotional turbulence of Friedrich Nietzsche's aphorisms "I am dead because I am stupid" and "I am stupid because I am dead." I glean my mortality mostly when I pronounce myself stupid to myself. Stupidity does not stand in opposition to wisdom or knowing, but rather stands by and for the prospect of owning knowledge. Or – having power over knowledge. Either one knows too much, which leaves no room for any alternative reading, any alternative possibility, or one knows not enough in order to remain perfectly latched to another reductive, bigoted narrative. Stupidity invites all kinds of social death. From snorting the wrong line to letting anti-Semitism creep in. "Coming to power is a costly business," Nietzsche writes, "power *makes stupid*."

☉

Prozac is one hell of a drug.

⊙

Depression is just anger without enthusiasm.

⊙

Now that I feel a bit better about myself, I am less suicidal. It distressed me at first, to have that much distance from my own death. Kill yourself internally before capitalism kills you externally.

⊙

When I did not feel better, I had a desire to get rid of "it." Poetry is the best weapon for wiping "it" out with fewer casualties, which is why poetry is never enough.

⊙

Sometimes "it" is "I," and sometimes "I" is "it." The process of removal is neither always clear nor precise. I want it to be the root of the problem so badly there will be no side effects, no consequences, other than that the truth of all relations will be revealed with its abolition.

⊙

I turn to self-abolition, which draws on a particular kind of death of the subject. This death successfully strips away those aspects of the subject as conditioned and subsumed by and within white supremacist, patriarchal capitalism. This is not to entertain the notion of an "outside" of white supremacist, patriarchal capitalism, but to take seriously the idea of radically shifting and removing conditioned behaviours and actions.

⊙

I wonder if "it" acts the part of the *Iliad*'s Muses in "IT MAKES ME ILIAD." If Muses are called upon to tell the story, if Muses rub the fore knuckle that grips the pen …

⊙

I cannot transcend the conditions that engender "it"; because of this limited sense of agency, the capacity to imagine a world where I am not ideologically pinned down feels like an impossibility. The task is not to identify with the structural role allotted me by power. Look over there, there "it" is.

⊙

I never liked aligning with my own Greekness. My mother is half Greek. As a teenager I remember Greek men telling me what to do. Grow your hair. Do not dye it that colour. Do not pierce your ears. You are rolling that joint wrong.

⊙

Poem IV. I aligned with my Greekness on December 6, 2008, when Alexandros Grigoropoulos, a fifteen-year-old student, was killed by police. "Merry Christmas From Athens" read a postcard with Christmas tree ablaze.

⊙

The giving of Christmas trees was often associated with the end of hostilities.

⊙

In the first half of the first millennium BCE, ancient Greek city states, most of which were maritime powers, began to look beyond Greece for land and resources and founded colonies across the Mediterranean.

⊙

Dark green indicates colonies that either were, or originated from, land controlled by the Dutch West India Company, light green the Dutch East India Company.

⊙

The French dreamed of replicating the wealth of Spain by colonizing tropical zones.

⊙

It is only by way of stripping, peeling back, destroying parts of the sovereign "I" that the subject is enabled to relate back to itself.

⊙

It is quite appealing to be rid of yourself on paper. Self-abolition in poetry ascribes a figurative death while you still persist in spirit. It is only the death of a certain kind of subject, the death of a fantasy, of the attempt to kill it.

⊙

It is a privilege when white poets try to abolish a category, like "the self" or "the poet," they have already mastered.

⊙

Poem v. Avital Ronell addressed graduate students on writing a dissertation: "Forget about your grandiose ego, bloated fantasies. You're a piece of shit." Tell that superego to quiet now, if not to completely shut the fuck up, that voice that is telling you "You are a piece of shit." Write before that voice confirms your inherited shittiness. Before she tells you no.

⊙

In September 2017, Avital Ronell was accused of sexual harassment by a student. Avital Ronell states these are false accusations. And I want to believe her. I really do, because of how misogynistic academia can be and is. Men have been doing this for years. That isn't an excuse, but it's an additional complication. The headlines glommed on to her perceived identity as a "Lesbian Feminist" in an attempt to nullify the validity of the #metoo movement. Here lies a destroyed illusion: yes, "Lesbian Feminists" can cause harm.

⊙

I can cause harm, and so does it.

⊙

The founders of American research universities were mainly inspired by German models.

⊙

If I am to stay monogamous with a text, as Avital Ronell suggests, and this same text rapes me in my sleep, am I allowed to file for divorce from it? Get ugly with that text like you would in any abusive relationship. That text was my tool. I loved that tool.

⊙

"Of course a hammer also falls under the idea of a political tool, and one can always do more than philosophize with it; one can make it sing or cry," writes Avital Ronell. The news of the accusations against Ronell makes me neither sing nor cry. I hold onto the news. To what the accused would later convince me was a kind of distorted attention to mass media.

⊙

I invited Avital Ronell to blurb *JUST LIKE I LIKE IT*, because her work helped shape my work, and it would be disingenuous to say it won't continue to do so. I have no answers other than it's necessary to hold all messy contradictions in tandem. Such a task is possible for me in poetry more than in an essay, let alone in this notes section, let alone in a complicated invitation to someone I admire to blurb, if not brand, if not blur, the back of this book.

⊙

A contradiction does not mean that holding incompatible feelings and thoughts in tandem implies the validity or equal weight of incompatible feelings and thoughts.

⊙

I can't disavow this shit. I can't disavow mendacious assumptions. I can't disavow horrible people. I can't disavow my own toxicity. I can't disavow my fine mind. I can't disavow irony. I can't disavow my stupidity. I can't disavow participating in the destruction of a subversive intellectual woman. I can't disavow naively yearning for this book to hold it all, both stained reputations and deep admiration. I can't disavow it not making any difference. I can't disavow texts altering consciousness. I can't disavow wasting time. And I refuse to do so. Thank you for your consideration.

⊙

In poem VI, I reference the musical *Chicago*. "Cell Block Tango" welcomes the "six merry murderesses of the Cook County Jail" repeating "Pop. Six. Squish. Uh uh. Cicero. Lipschitz!" In book VI of the *Iliad*, Hector reassures his wife that no one will hurl his body down to Hades unless it is fated. Unless he "has it coming." I think men, and the man inside my head, have it coming. I am willing to lose half an audience over this thought.

⊙

In poem VII, I reference Cassius's address to Brutus in Shakespeare's *Julius Caesar*: "The fault, dear Brutus, is not in our stars, / But in ourselves, that we are underlings." The sun sets, yes, but this does not mean you wake up with its rise.

⊙

In poem VII, after you rape her, I no longer read your poems. I no longer read your materials, but continue to text you.

⊙

I hoped change was only as new as a new season.

⊙

Poem VII. I assemble reflections on Lyn Hejinian's "The Maddening of Connections" (from a longer project, *Positions of the Sun*), which was published in *Armed Cell* 3 (2012). I wrote and wailed these reflections the night before they were presented during a Kootenay School of Writing event, "I'm in you, you're in me." I went mad. This is not romantic. My mad ramblings were transcribed.

⊙

That night I learned about allegory.

⊙

As poets we have a conscious need to bring language into language; not necessarily to find something new, but instead to create a work that cannot be overheard. The divergence between political practice and poetry is in this continual tension between sense-making and the war on sensibility. The madness of relaying untruths (manufactured structures of control) in heroic history, which is the madness of poetry, does not always lend itself to the tactical clarity necessary for material action. But in her introduction to *The Language of Inquiry*, Hejinian states:

> But [poetry] is also a denotatively social and therefore political practice. Poetry comes to know that things are. But this is not knowledge in the strictest sense; it is rather, acknowledgment – and that constitutes a sort of unknowing. To know *that* things are is not to know *what* they are, and to know *that* without *what* is to know otherness (i.e., the unknown and perhaps unknowable). Poetry undertakes acknowledgment as a preservation of otherness – a notion that can be offered in a political, as well as an epistemological, context.

⊙

Poetry can document not only truths about exploitation and oppression, a literal reading of what the state supplies in terms of social realities and experience, but can also unknow, and make available our own subject to the work, so that we can both experience the oppression to which we've been anesthetized and unmake it.

⊙

At the time I had a hard time with prepositions.

⊙

Poem VIII. I hold onto a particular narrative about roast beef: There is an image in one of my baby books featuring my dad, his biological mom, and my mother's adopted parents, my Grammie and Grampie. They are clinking glasses filled with red wine in celebration of a new baby, me. They are about to scarf my mother's home cooking, her roast beef. It upsets me to no end imagining that my mother made this roast beef without any help from any of these people.

⊙

Poem VIII. After I spent some time in the Bay Area in 2015, I had consumed just enough New Age spiritualism to seek out a psychic. (This same psychic told a friend she was cursed.) I gave the psychic my money. The psychic told me I used to be a bad man. An alchemist, a healer, but nonetheless a bad man. I told the psychic about roast beef. The psychic made an adjustment to my narrative: while yes, my mother is absent in the image, she too is celebrating just as much as they are. She prepared a meal in celebration, just like she prepared a new baby. I am satisfied considering my mother is temporarily made whole.

⊙

Poem IX. Spain is still on Nazi time. Francisco Franco changed March 16, 1940, 23:00 Greenwich Mean Time to March 17, 1940, 00:00 Central European Time. This time-zone change was made permanent in 1942, so as to be in accord with German-occupied Europe.

⊙

Jeff Derksen's watch tells Communist time.

⊙

Poem X. Louis Althusser murdered Hélène Rytmann, his wife. He strangled her. He describes the murder in the aptly titled *The Future Lasts Forever*:

> Hélène, also in a dressing-gown, lay before me on her back. Her pelvis was resting on the edge of the bed, her legs dangled on the carpet. Kneeling beside her, leaning across her body, I was massaging her neck. I would often silently massage the nape of her neck and her back. I had learnt the technique as a prisoner-of-war from little Clerc, a professional footballer who was an expert

at all sorts of things. But on this occasion I was massaging the front of her neck. I pressed my thumbs into the hollow at the top of her breastbone and then, still pressing, slowly moved them both, one to the left, the other to the right, up toward her ears where the flesh was hard. I continued massaging her in a V-shape. The muscles in my forearms began to feel very tired; I was aware that they always did when I was massaging.

⊙

I used to wail at an ex, "Make 'it' stop," as though it were a symbiotic parasitic feeling crawling through my insides.

⊙

I am so lonely now without it. I am so full now without an ex.

⊙

Depression, like ideology, can lie to you – it can tell you that you are the only one experiencing it. Perhaps the source of my attention to Althusser-the-wife-murderer over the years is that I can visualize him rubbing his way out of something to the detriment of his wife's subject, her breath. Her life. I think he killed her in order to free himself of himself. Self-abolition did not contribute to this opening, but violence against women did. The cultural and social stakes of the persisting, self-annihilating subject are precisely when it reproduces the misogyny and racism of such great theorists.

⊙

I wish she had pressed her thumbs into the hollow at the top of his breastbone.

⊙

One early morning my lover consensually choked me. I whispered, "Do it," but I do not think my lover heard me. I whispered it in such a way my lover would not be able to hear it: "Do it, just kill me already. Get me over with."

⊙

Poem XII. The gameplay moves are a mixture of *Mortal Kombat* finishing moves and *Call of Duty* ones. In *Friendly + Fire* I reference the letter "f" as a pleasurable letter, or a soft letter, a soft-sounded letter, until -ucked.

◉

"Fuck" is not derived from Old English roots, but it still plays a flexible role in English, and this is why I love it.

◉

Poem XV. Deanna Fong is a Brazilian jiu-jitsu goddess. She can choke me out any day.

◉

Poem XVI. The Gods contemplate defying fate in order to save their children's fate.

◉

Poem XVI. I used to draw secret assassins. Some had a special tattoo, a symbol, on the right of their face, others on their forearm. These assassins, these women, were always dressed for battle. I think of these assassins as I put my armour on, with RuPaul in the background demanding "Don't fuck it up. It is time to lip-sync for your life."

◉

Poem XVII. I posted a picture on Instagram of an excerpt of Magdalena Zurawski's *Companion Animal* while in Spain. My painted black toes are in the frame too:

> When I was a public
> property the librarian
> shooed the homeless
> from my ribcage. She said,
> "This is not a shelter." I said,
> "But I am a public
>
> property."

⊙

Poem XVII. I write ████████ an email:

Subject: *hola. no entiendo.*

May 15, 2017, 10:35, to ██████

What does it mean that when work is referred to as abject, or aligned with a common practice with self-identified women poets, I recoil. I wrote my thesis on this very thing, this tendency for "younger" women writers to pervert the page like it's a body, focusing on ██████ and ██████. I wrote about them both because I consumed their work quickly, too quickly. I'm attaching the document in question, because why not?

I received your letter and was excited. and I then I felt self-conscious: I don't want to be lumped into this category of women writers, even if it looks like I've lumped myself into it voluntarily. My first book cut off the subject completely. with this new book I'm going to use it more conservatively than *F+F* – so *JUST LIKE I LIKE IT* will be like a mama bear book, just right.

I'm in Spain now on residency. I need your address. If you are feeling ambitious this is the address here: Carril del Parra, 8, 30160 La Cueva, Murcia. I arrived yesterday after too many hours of travel. I woke up from a siesta and thought it was the next day, the next year. a stray cat just passed me. I leave on May 29. Too soon.

I'm writing two new sections of *JLILI* – one called «IT MAKES ME ILIAD,» written in very fashionable dactylic hexameter. erín moure once told me, a number of years ago in Lithuania, that I «had a funny way of pronouncing things.» ████████████████████████████ The word in question was APLOMB.

The last section, "ACTION PANTIES," will take the form of adventures in soap boxing. Today I walked through the small town and scouted locations where I'll set up.

I haven't talked to my friend yet. If I write too much on this topic I'll start to re-hate myself. So I'll leave it at that.

I brought your books with me. ████████████████████████

but now I don't.

I wrote half a poem and then siestaed before I could think: Why are you doing this? The doing being the writing. If I didn't write I'd die. I'm dying everyday, but when I write poems I'm perfectly dead. I don't want to write: alive.

I have a house in Greece. It's my biological uncle's house. I travelled there in 2014. I was losing my mind before the trip (before before the trip) and likely should not have been travelling. It was just me in the house. I'm having that moment right now like when I'm with my therapist: I tell him I wish I could project a video rather than say anything. You are not my therapist, don't worry, but I'm being honest: I wish I could send you a video from then.

I initially mentioned the house because I want to hold a residency there for a month. There's enough space for six, I think. I want to hold a residency there every other year in the spring. It's in Malamata. Population 150 in the summer.

I'm trailing. I'm listing. Listless.

Here's a song: https://www.youtube.com/watch?v=euiKqmLvyMw&list =PLAluFTURxRMPoRiETYfyliVnEBrfaotjE&index=4

Currently: perfectly alive. Breathing and knowing it.

Soon,
Danielle

⊙

Poem XX. ██████████ introduces rape apologist Laura Kipnis on May 3, 2017. I shout "PUSSY" after ██████ replaces █████'s words with the watered down "gratuitous word." Grab them by the "gratuitous word" just doesn't account for the violence implicit of ████████████'s speech.

⊙

████████ writes a lot on social media about victimization and political correctness and the rational left. He is not into call-out culture. I don't blame him. Call-out culture can really "hurt feelings." If only we could all be in the same room together and talk "rationally." Sob.

⊙

Poem XX. ████████ gave me a C– and it felt like a kiss.

⊙

Poem XX. Stan Lee and Jack Kirby used civil rights leaders Martin Luther King Jr. and Malcolm X as inspiration for the mutants Professor X and Magneto who first appeared in September 1963. Black Panther, the first black superhero, appeared in July 1966, and was originally named "Coal Tiger" by Jack Kirby.

⊙

Poem XXII. The two in question are Thelma and Louise. The two women smile at each other knowingly. They would rather die together than get caught in a cop web.

⊙

Poem XXII. Some of the items listed in this explosion are from Michelangelo Antonioni's 1970 film *Zabriskie Point*. The explosion is far more rewatchable than the orgy-for-two.

⊙

Poem XXIV. Present participles are incredibly unbecoming in a poem, or so we are taught, so here they are.

POWER BOTTOM'S DREAM

"POWER BOTTOM'S DREAM" hurts, because to contend with the subject's ideological construction, the speaking subject must be prepared to exorcise the damage and privileges it has enabled. It is not an interpretation but an embodiment of the speaking subject's relationship to power. While it manifests as both consensual and malignant parasites, it is difficult for the speaking subject to deny its effect on making her who she is and influencing who and what she loves and likes. When it is destroyed, will the speaking subject indeed be free and cleared from it? And is that the point?

⊙

Maria Lassnig's painting *You or Me* (2005) is a visual influence in "POWER BOTTOM'S DREAM." I saw the painting at New York's Metropolitan Museum of Art's *Unfinished* exhibition in early 2016. The naked figure points one gun at her temple and another at the audience, alternately blurring the distinction between murder and suicide, making and unmaking. For me it is the quintessential question: How to make plain ideology when it is smacking you in the face?

⊙

"POWER BOTTOM'S DREAM" strips some language from Catherine Millet's *The Sexual Life of Catherine M.* For example, the word "coccyx."

⊙

"POWER BOTTOM'S DREAM" was inspired by Arno Schmidt's 1970 novel, *Bottom's Dream*, topped by my own sexual proclivities.

⊙

"POWER BOTTOM'S DREAM" originally purged anger, sin, in order to be civilized.

⊙

"POWER BOTTOM'S DREAM" calls into question the manner in which one eats – how one eats is analogous to how one's body will perform other functions. What happens if the body is starved for nourishment? What if the body is un-energized, what then must it turn to in order to continue? The manner in which these eating and speaking bodies reside next to other speaking and eating bodies is called into question. What is the analogy between metabolism and communication? Does one metabolize the other in order to commune with them? Does the difference between *para* and *sitos* resonate something in the difference between bodies? Is a parasite a nearness or a oneness?

◉

"POWER BOTTOM'S DREAM" can become lubricated during sex as a defense mechanism against tearing and pain, regardless of one's level of enthusiasm or emotional buy-in.

◉

Sometimes fucking it out feels like a possibility.

◉

"POWER BOTTOM'S DREAM" is routinely insatiable.

◉

"POWER BOTTOM'S DREAM" does not depend on lovers to fuck it out anymore. Though it might have yesterday.

◉

I am haunted by the next time, not the last time.

◉

"POWER BOTTOM'S DREAM" is an insatiable romantic slut looking for the right "it."

◉

"POWER BOTTOM'S DREAM" famously gets its head transformed into that of an ass. If Bottom's head is that of an ass, then what can Bottom's ego produce other than shit?

⊙

"Hold on to your shit," declares the King. "Dispose of it only in the dark of night. Remove your pigs from sight beyond the city's walls, or I will seize your person and your goods, engulf your home in my capacious purse, and lock your body in my jail." The King, like the Emperor, wears no clothes which the court pretends to admire. The King, unlike the Proletariat, neither farts nor shits. The King needs an enema and these poems just squirted. We cannot digest nor shit without some kind of sustenance.

⊙

What does an ass dream?

⊙

"POWER BOTTOM'S DREAM" of power under, not power over.

⊙

A dreamer assumes the role of Bottom and yells, "You cannot fire me, I already quit." "You cannot break up with me, I never loved you" is the speech act of "POWER BOTTOM'S DREAM." "You cannot hit me, I am spanking myself" is another.

⊙

Butt, dear "POWER BOTTOM'S DREAM," while such utterances do carve out a bit of autonomy, they do not hold space for dreams without bounds. "The work of the bottom is never done," writes Cassandra Troyan. "The work of the bottom is also to spread the truths that only the bottom knows." I respond, "AND REACH BEYOND THE PRECIPICE, THE EDGE, THE LIMIT. AND TO TAKE THAT INTO EVERYDAY PRACTICE, ALWAYS READY FOR MORE THAN WHAT CAPITALISM DECLARES POSSIBLE." And they respond back, "STARTED FROM THE BOTTOM THAT ORIGINALLY SEEMED LIKE THE BOTTOM UNTIL YOU

REALIZED THERE ARE INFINITE BOTTOMS BEYOND THAT BOTTOM." And I respond back, "BETWEEN A BOTTOM AND A HARD PLACE."

And I continue here: The power bottom widens their sphere for action, holding in their bodies a submission not endured anywhere else but where they want it.

⊙

Asking whether or not they know what they actually want is the wrong question. The right one is, rather, a statement: They know what they want. So fucking bad, it hurts. Few of us are prepared to say that we like that too.

IT SOUNDS LIKE A SMALL SCUM

I wrote an unsent letter to Ann Cvetkovich that was initially to be read in front of my classmates for a graduate course on performance and the archive. I did not attend the class, nor did I read the letter in front of classmates. I am trying to muster up adequate language for why I was not in attendance other than I was stuck in the fetal position with too many taunting fragments.

Monday, November 3, 2014

Dear Ann,

The public component of this letter, oddly enough, is off-putting. I would like to find a mode of address that is intimate but not nauseating for our witnesses. In part I must determine how to meld my previous exposure to your work with this current iteration. When I read through your "Depression Journals" over the summer, they prompted me to move. "When the brain is vacant, or shut down, or endlessly fearful, there's something reassuring about showing signs of physical life." Your writing was the best therapy, and it prompted me to closely consider the impasse and my impasse. It turned into a conference paper; it turned into a performance. A call for help in the guise of academic rigour?

I subordinated my preference for making this all about me to my preference for something in between. "There's nothing new, really, except ice and rain. Environmental dissolubility" (█ to me, 2008) – I have to reference a partner in

138

order to find space to address you. Not my words. Where I stumbled: the lesbian archive as an archive of emotion and trauma and how this archive exposes both an affective response to global crisis and an affective response to small everyday cuts.

An anonymous friend enters the anonymous gallery. His speech wavers, his eyes glossy. He breaks down. Another anonymous friend witnesses the exact moment when his private feelings are exposed in public and escorts said friend into the back room. Later that week, this intuitive friend tells me: "When emotions are expressed in public, no longer contained in the enclave of the mind, the house, the seriousness of the situation is revealed and made visible." I was at first jealous, but I'm sad too. Notice me too.

At this moment, I've had to stop. I'm at a café and there are flies landing on my screen. Free-floating signifiers and half-constructed sentences. On the one hand, it is inspiring to acknowledge feelings and to consider the archive of emotion and trauma as "affectively motivated by the passionate desire to claim the fact of history" and to place value on every piece of material "a lesbian considers critical in her life." But (and this isn't necessarily a comment intended to counter the above) what interpersonal dynamics need to be in place in order for this to function? To feel quote-unquote safe? It isn't only a matter of constructing the space with restrictions on gender or sexuality, as normative boundaries (white, heteronormative, patriarchal) can be reproduced within these social sites, but of accounting for the ugliness and messiness that erupts when contending with everyone's feelings as equally worthwhile. This can lead to feeling unsafe. I understand how difficult it is to write about these intricacies. Those hidden, unshaped moments of living are the personal and relational sites where emotional labour is located. To then locate it in an actual location – this Brownstone or that basement, the unconscious – is important in times when precarity and immateriality are maddening. Sometimes you need to see the parasite in order to kill it. Sometimes you need to touch something just to feel a fleeting glimpse of wholeness.

Isn't there a political necessity to not have these archives situated in the institution, so that some kind of fiction around the last refuge, an outside, could possibly be felt even if it's not real? Isn't there something about the institution that feeds into the factual truth, or legitimization, over affective capacities? What do you think about how easily bodies and feelings can be captured by neoliberalized modes of therapy and made comprehensible in order for social subjects to continue functioning as productive "good citizens" and workers?

Your work initially relieved me, as it provided a theoretical pattern to align both knowing and feeling, but now I'm thinking more specifically about how expressing feelings in public are misconstrued as an individuated act. Public outbursts – though telling and serious and humiliating – involve the individual and witnesses. All are affected. While the depressive internally falls apart, she solders herself to the notion that she knows the truth and is the only one knowing and seeing and feeling it. She becomes a reductive spectacle when the ego dominates as such. That is, if there isn't a ground where humiliation and stupidity and depression aren't honestly thought of as bound together, addressed in tandem, then the ego's domination only estranges the depressive from people and anything left of sincerity in more personal projects (e.g., a book of poems, essays, a painting).

In her blog post "Selfcare as Warfare," Sara Ahmed attempts to reconcile the often neoliberalized and individuated mode of self-care with political depression. She alludes to the everyday and the tiny cuts that make up the whole experience of living under the logic of capitalism and exploitation: "But to assume people's ordinary ways of coping with injustices implies some sort of failure on their part – or even an identification with the system – is another injustice they have to cope with … You might not be trying to move up, to project yourself forward; you might simply be trying not to be brought down. Heavy, heavy histories. Wearing, worn down" (*feministkilljoys.com*). A rebellion itself is always diagnosable. I stick my feeling in the *DSM* and come up empty. There is no outside, so how do you live in it and with it while at the same time resisting any inclination to live in it and with it? Isn't the refusal to participate bestowing the structure with too much power that only enables the social subject to continue to be stuck? No, refusal is power. It is how you perform refusal within those tiny cuts, from never writing "just a friendly reminder" to hitting a cop with an umbrella.

There was a ten-year gap between *An Archive of Feelings: Trauma, Sexuality, and Lesbian Public Cultures* and *Depression: A Public Feeling*. Is an archive of feeling a solution or an alternative to medical models? And what measures need to be in place in order for feelings not to be threatened by categorization, attributed to medical models, while also making something visible and real so that we're not completely numb and overwhelmed, isolated, by an archive of feelings? There is a type of counter-public you're talking about here – it's specific to the LGBTQ2+ communites. The specific social site, the specific communities, with all their differences, need to be even further established, otherwise we run into the appropriateion of the subaltern, the "third space," the "undercommons," etc. What if a straight white man took up his feelings in the way you're describing? Would we empathize with his gross display? A friend tells me how women are trained to be compassionate at the sight of another's feelings, and that this is why women stay in abusive relationships. The visible sign of tears means something deeper. Feelings can be weaponized. Feelings are not pure truth – I think this is why I am uncertain about your emphasis on affective truth / factual truth. How do we think about feelings as having equal value? But what happens when the individual is lost, dissolved, amidst the fray of others coming to terms with their own feelings? Some feelings are grosser than others. And not all privileges are equal.

An anonymous friend and I walk Iona Beach. Industrial waste, shit and beauty, airport. We talk about this letter to you and I mention how important fantasy is, if only for the sake of imagining something different, whether personally or collectively. I express my worry about still succumbing to the logic of knowing. That we can only validate the feeling by making it known and concrete. Like when she's asked, "But how do you know you were raped?"

A flock of birds turn in such a way that they become invisible. Is this to keep away the predators or to play a trick on their prey? We decide it's both and grin at each other mischievously. Oh, to be both visible and invisible!

And what of the body? The body that is already decaying, dying, then led further to its ending by way of state violence, racialized violence, the police. And what of the theory of the body? The academic rigour that goes into deciphering the failed body, the moving body, the ill-equipped-to-quit body. I am concerned about what sitting in the classroom did to my body. I bought a kneeling chair so now I'm forced to pray.

During her seminar held at SFU Harbour Centre, Rebecca Schneider made reference to her ability to articulate; she had acquired the ability to pontificate in a way that forcefully conveys a message to the listener. From a preface about her laboured voice (the opposite of voicelessness), she then became excited about the potentiality of what she framed as "a purposeful error." (And as an aside, the relentless manner in which "the failure" [i.e., failure to write a poem that moves, failure to be an ally and support the ones you love, the failure inherent to whiteness] transmutes into a new contemporary problem: failure has become a replacement for guilt. And we all know guilt is a worthless emotion, as it disconnects us from our bodies.) Schneider, referencing [I can't remember the reference], said that "groping" is how we come into our gestures and our embodied skill sets through errors. Then – she reached for her water bottle and missed, using *this* as a concrete example of purposeful error, of failure. No – failure is when you try to reach for that bottle and unintentionally miss it. Slight panic. Gleam of sweat. You're found out. You hope no one has seen the tremor in your hand. This tremor is private. Not shared. No potential.

I wonder if the emphasis on public feelings is so that we/I don't become enveloped by individuated and internalized melancholia. Colectivo Situaciones write about how "sadness consists in being separated from our powers (*potencias*). Among us political sadness often took the form of impotence." After the movement and the protest are over there is work that needs to be done so that I/we don't just fall back into old, individuated habits. So that we collectively create the conditions that shrink the distance between the "social experiment" and the "political imagination capable of carrying it out."

You mention something about words without words. You mention fantasy and Jean Carlomusto's hunch, an exhibit of feeling something before you can know it. Is her use of fantasy and constructed fiction around her family a part of this interstitial work between everyday experience and political movement? I wonder how assembling fragmented histories and emotional memories into something that is very concrete (a video, an exhibition, an archive) will always be a work of fiction. The fantasy. The long ongoingness – is this a kind of slowness the body needs but is persistently denied? The fiction is how the past could become apparent/savoured. The document is a part of the archive, and *activates* it through affect, experience, sense, more than through its mere existence.

I am told Greeks invented emotions and democracy and homosexuality. Do I want to mention how I swam in the Mediterranean with your book sitting next to me? Do I want to indulge in this fantasy of how I read you and didn't read you, I just needed you near? The cover was the same turquoise as the sea keeping me buoyant.

xxo,
Danielle

ACTION PANTIES

"ACTION PANTIES" masticates what were going to be epigraphs for *JUST LIKE I LIKE IT*. Roger Farr reminded me that giving the epigraphs the beginning, the entryway into the book, is like giving the writers of said epigraphs too much prime real estate.

"ACTION PANTIES" gloms on to the language of Mehdi Haeri Yazdi ("In the anatomy of knowledge, 'I' and 'IT' make up a unity of opposition"), Clarice Lispector

("Fear that it all, like when a button is pressed [...] would start working noisily, mechanically, filling the rooms with movements and sounds, living"), Anita Phillips ("The encounter ends not with apotheosis, but orgasm. The story is about spending rather than saving. If the world is a violent, mean and sordid place, the masochist rejects transcendence as a way of handling it"), Avital Ronell ("Sometimes the state has a hand in it"), and Walid Raad ("I no longer know if it is real").

◉

The title, "ACTION PANTIES," pays homage to Valie Export's 1968 performance in Munich, later exhibited as "Action Pants: Genital Panic." She sits on a bench against a wall of doors, legs spread, wearing crotchless trousers and a leather shirt, holding a machine gun. While experimental filmmakers showed their work, Export positioned her exposed, hairy pussy at eye level, challenging women's historical representation as passive objects denied and devoid of agency.

◉

Many versions of the performance have been mythologized both by the audience and by the artist.

◉

In Murcia I scouted locations for my own performance. I wanted to soapbox with no one to hear. That's a lie. It was captured. I came across a seemingly abandoned shack with "PAIN" graffitied on steel panelling. I didn't expose my hairy pussy like Export. At this point, I mused, what's the point I am trying to make? I wore a virginal-esque white nightie in broad daylight with brand developer Jessa Carter documenting for her own project on Clarice Lispector. Export wanted "to be provocative, to provoke" and I wanted to wear all white with no audience other than Carter "to be vague" with my intentions for being there. I stood on a brick, barefoot. I waited for a defiant gesture to take hold and usher in a new event.

◉

There is always something unsaid, undone, yet to be said, yet to be done. Sometimes it is a placeholder for everything inarticulable, everything undone, everything unsaid. All reduced to a non-referential, lifeless subject. I sound more morose than

I intend to. Is my concern about not making enough noise or not making the right noise? I am thinking about what it means to start with Valie Export as a reference and where that reference ended up. I am thinking about whether or not I missed the mark, the bull's eye, if it had concluded differently, maybe with more visible, hairy pussy, "it" would have been said, done, articulated. Rather a placeholder, "it" takes off its sunglasses and reveals what is really meant to be drawn to this and wind up that.

I MIGHT DIE BEFORE I LIKE IT

A list poem felt and still feels like a cheap trick. Like a mantra, either exorcising or creating distance from a thought or a feeling.

⊙

"I MIGHT DIE BEFORE I LIKE IT" offered repetition to me as a container, a playpen, I can freely play madly within.

⊙

"I MIGHT DIE BEFORE I LIKE IT" is a mouth full with piss-poor flow.

⊙

"I MIGHT DIE BEFORE I LIKE IT" embraces the title of Walid Raad's 1993 photograph series, *I might die before I get a rifle.*

⊙

"I MIGHT DIE BEFORE I LIKE IT" examines and documents ammunitions.

⊙

"I MIGHT DIE BEFORE I LIKE IT" provides a bit of distance for the poet and something consumptive for the reader. The form is an obvious container for loose language. What does it mean now that it is contained in a list? Does it need to be listed?

◉

The list sometimes keeps a beat, a momentum. I turn to list poems, to repetition, when I need to stay grounded within my own work, within my brand of function creep.

◉

The list keeps me in line.

◉

"I MIGHT DIE BEFORE I LIKE IT" prompts my stepmom to question whether I like all the things listed, which prompts us to discuss what it even means to like a thing. If a thing is liked too quickly, it means it is consumed too quickly, the speed of which deletes any tensions or negativity.

◉

I remember the origin of "I MIGHT DIE BEFORE I LIKE IT." Amy De'ath and Sean O'Brien were leaving town and hosted a soiree along with a reading by friends. I pilfered lines from Amy's poems, admixed with my own, and had people drink anytime they recognized Amy's lines.

◉

"I MIGHT DIE BEFORE I LIKE IT" tips its hat to death.

◉

There are ways of writing that damage. My experience of writing is as a release, but also abject in the sense that I often do not want to look at it. I could more easily dissect a shit then return to a piece of writing. Any vagaries are a result of a fear around looking. Like the effects of a hangover.

I wonder if Eve Sedgwick was able to write in the way she did because she was on the verge of death. I reiterate another way: I trust her writing, even her references to yoga and Buddhism, because she is dead. Just now I wonder if I have brought myself to the precipice of death while writing so that I will finally look at my words and satisfy myself. Supine scriptum asphyxiation.

"I MIGHT DIE BEFORE I LIKE IT" struggles against a state of inertia. The most successful feeling is movement of the body. "When the brain is vacant," Cvetkovich writes, "or shut down, or endlessly fearful, there's something reassuring about showing signs of physical life." In the summer of 2014, I read this line of prose situated under the heading "Swimming" and immediately rode my bicycle to Second Beach pool. Empty, free of conversation and social relations. "The rhythm of breathing and the ease of the strokes keep my body flowing," Cvetkovich continues in her "Depression Memoir," "and, with it, my mind. With the breathing, panic subsides somewhat and it's possible to think again."

Swimming involves oscillating between the panic-stricken state outside the water and the panicked rhythm of breath underwater. Physiologically, "rapid, shallow breathing can cause hypoxia and a buildup of carbon dioxide in the [blood]" and panic consumes the swimmer, hindering the ability to solve problems. A heart attack.

"I MIGHT DIE BEFORE I LIKE IT" read from a "How to Dive" article on SportDive. com that scores of dead divers are recovered with working equipment, plenty of air, and their weight belts firmly in place; most experts believe that death due to panic is far more common than previously reported …

To redeem my earlier dismissal of list poems as "cheap tricks," I see my list as an uncategorized inventory. There is a logic, but it is more a means to maintain focus, maintain discipline.

◉

"I MIGHT DIE BEFORE I LIKE IT" is the perfect formal trick for a power bottom who comes into what she likes by doing and being done to.

◉

Raad writes of his images, "These situations of extreme violence can produce new ways of assimilating the data of the world, new ways of living, experiencing, feeling the world." In a control society I do not want my agency to be constantly suspect. Rather than inspect a compartmentalized piece of artillery, how could this lemon I'm holding and squeezing in my left hand be weaponized? How could I experience this lemon differently than whatever that last question aroused in me? With this lemon I can make you a salad, with this lemon I can squirt juice into your wound so you can feel that much more than before.

◉

"I MIGHT DIE BEFORE I LIKE IT" can either be interpreted as acceptable or unacceptable desires. Or something completely different, like curious or actionable desires.

◉

"I MIGHT DIE BEFORE I LIKE IT" is not interested in reaching for a silver lining. But sometimes, red canna lilies flower seventy-five years later.

ACKNOWLEDGMENTS

JUST LIKE I LIKE IT was conceived and developed on the stolen and occupied Lands of the xʷməθkʷəy̓əm, Sḵwx̱wú7mesh, and səlilwətaʔɬ Peoples.

"JUST LIKE I LIKE IT," or "JLILI," is a coinage from friends Dina Gonzalez and Joelle Ciona. To you both: I like you for knowing just what you like. Over drinks we excitedly talked about the idea of the book titled *JUST LIKE I LIKE IT*, with Dina producing drawings. Dina knows exactly what I like.

During the month of May 2017, I spent two weeks in Murcia, Spain, for La Postiza's "Endless Obsession" residency. Here I submitted to a reoccurring theme, repeating it again and again. Always and always. And always. "IT MAKES ME ILIAD" truly came to life in the tiny artist house beside a lemon grove. Thank you to Belén Conesa for your hospitality and to Jessa Carter for endless conversations about Clarice Lispector (the true voice of obsession), for music, and for lemon rituals.

Excerpts of *JUST LIKE I LIKE IT* were published in *The Capilano Review, Armed Cell,* and *Capitalism Nature Socialism.* A French translation of "IT MAKES ME ILIAD" by Simon Brown, "Trois Poèmes Extraits de 'IT MAKES ME ILIAD,'" was published in *Watts,* an online poetry journal based in Marseille; a Spanish translation of "IT MAKES ME ILIAD" by Olga Garcia, "ME HACES ILIADA," was published in *La Presa*; and a Slovenian translation of "POWER BOTTOM'S DREAM," "MOČ ZAD-NJJIČHNIH SANJ (odlomek)" in the literary journal *IDIOT*.

To Catriona Strang, ryan fitzpatrick, Roger Farr, and Deanna Fong for always taking the work seriously and often seeing what I am doing with a kind of opaque clarity I need and welcome.

To Olga Garcia for our emphatic correspondence and translations of our poems and our lives. And our broken, rotting teeth.

To the texts that shape and continue to shape me. Even to the ones I have exorcised from my shelves.

And to those for whom I feel forever deeply, who inspired this book as sirens, never muses: Andrea Actis, Tim Atkins, Anahita Jamali Rad, Alexis Baker, Sarah Tarcea, Holly Chemirika, Megan Hepburn, Erica Holt, Alex Muir, Maria Wallstam, Natalie Knight, Dianna Bonder, Dorothy Trujillo Lusk, Haida Antolick, Aaron Vidaver, Reg Johanson, Rachel Zolf, Jeff Derksen, Samantha Giles, Stephanie Young, Ted Byrne, Aja Moore, Ben Hynes, CAConrad, Shawna Delgaty, Anna Ruddick, Amy De'Ath, Sean O'Brien, Cassandra Troyan, Ted Rees, Alessandra Capperdoni,

Magdalena Zurawski, my darling garbage person, Josh Rose, and my co-worker family at nə́ćaʔmat ct Strathcona Branch and CUPE 391.

And, always, to Honey, my mom, my dad, my stepmom, my stepsister, and the gem of my life, my sister, Jeunesse LaFrance.

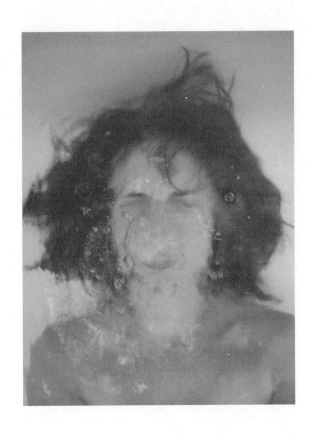

DANIELLE LaFRANCE lives on occupied and stolen xʷməθkʷəy̓əm, Sḵwx̱wú7mesh, and səlilwətaʔɬ Lands. She is a poet, community librarian, fighter, and independent scholar, among other things, venusian, anarcha-feminist, stupid …

She is the author of *species branding* (CUE 2010), *Friendly + Fire* (Talonbooks 2016), and the chapbook *Pink Slip* (SIC 2013).

She is committed to listening, addressing, and responding to the radical root of things.

Her favourite colour is purple.

Her favourite smell is *péché*.

Her favourite word is no.